D1268461

GOLF ... *it's a funny game*

GOLF

... it's a funny game

David Scaletti

Lothian
BOOKS

Thomas C. Lothian Pty Ltd
132 Albert Road, South Melbourne, Victoria 3205
www.lothian.com.au

Photographs and captions copyright © David Scaletti 2004
Text copyright © David Scaletti 2004
www.sportscapes.com
First published 2004

All rights reserved. No part of this publication may be reproduced,
stored in a retrieval system or transmitted in any form by any means
without the prior permission of the copyright owner.
Enquiries should be made to the publisher.

Scaletti, David.
    Golf : it's a funny game.

    ISBN 0 7344 0738 6.

    1. Golf - Miscellanea. 2. Golf - Humor. 3. Golf -
    Quotations, maxims, etc. 4. Golfers - Quotations. I.
    Title.

796.35202

Cover and text design by Andrew Cunningham – Studio Pazzo
Typeset by Andrew Cunningham – Studio Pazzo
Printed and bound in China by Everbest Printing Co Ltd

FRONT COVER IMAGE The Royal Melbourne Golf Club, Hole 11, West Course, Par 4
PRECEDING SPREAD Kooyonga Golf Club, Australia. Hole 17, Par 4
FOLLOWING SPREAD Royal Dornoch Golf Club, Scotland. Hole 8, Par 4

To all golfers who believe that they can do better tomorrow … or the next day.

Golf for most of us, is an exercise in futility. An opportunity to wallow in our delusional belief that we really can play the game. From time to time it actually happens. We hit the perfect drive, follow up with a laser accurate approach shot, and massage the long curling putt into the bottom of the cup. Each shot an exquisite display of our golfing pedigree. Unfortunately, these shots are supposed to occur one after the other, not on a random or annual basis. But like true believers we maintain our practise of the ritual, hoping our blind faith and dedication will bring about a miraculous transformation. Despite overwhelming evidence to the contrary.

Now and then this steadfast faith in a good and just God of Golf is rewarded with a near perfect game. But we know we can do that little bit better. If only we practised more. Tried harder. Could relax. Had a personal coach. An Eastern Guru. A new set of clubs. A new hat. A new glove. Anything!

Yes . . . it's a never-ending cycle of ecstasy, frustration, anger, pleasure and hope. Just like life really, but much more important.

Lahinch Golf Club, Ireland. Hole 6, Par 4

My game at Lahinch was memorable for all the wrong reasons. Near gale force winds, driving rain and a thorough soaking, despite my waterproof gear, was hard going to say the least. The weather had not improved when I returned later with a camera, but then what would be the use of a postcard-perfect day when I'd just braved the toughest of conditions? This image aptly reflects my day's golf and reminds me what a great course Lahinch is.

Most people play golf for the first time out of curiosity.
Every time thereafter they are motivated purely by revenge.

DAVID FEHERTY

Ellerston Golf Course,
Australia. Hole 13, Par 4

I usually attempt to find
my shot from the
perspective of the golfer,
but this panoramic bush
view some distance from
the players' customary
path was irresistible.
Unmistakably Australian.

When I first became involved in golf course design I had the pleasure and distinction of working alongside the great Pete Dye. He commented with clarity and distinction that 'golfers love to be punished'. I wholeheartedly agree, and believe it is true across the board: male, female, amateur or professional. I also believe the work of every golf course designer, past and present, embodies that sentiment to some degree.

GREG NORMAN

Friar's Head Golf Club,
USA. Hole 10, Par 3

I love the peace and
solitude of a golf course as I
wait for the light to be right,
though it can get lonely on
occasion. Conversation is a
great way to pass the time
and with the sun coming
up on a setting as lovely as
the 10th, and a fellow
enthusiast to share it with,
all that was missing was a
good cup of coffee
and a biscuit.

One's golf may be of the placid type or of the stormy/tempestuous type;
I have experienced both, and I'll take either one.

BEN CRENSHAW

Splashes of contrasting colour
are a gift to the photographer
and here the long dry grass
provided an ideal visual
ingredient. A day later it had
all but disappeared, leaving
one less problem for the golfer
and a photographer extremely
grateful to have followed his
instincts and seized
the moment.

I'm the best. I just haven't played yet.

Muhammad Ali

Often the photographer in me
will take over from the golfer.
When I spot a cloud bank like
this wafting majestically over
the course, it becomes a mad
scramble finding a suitable
hole to capture the scene on
film. But you'll find most
golfers rarely comment on
such passing phenomena; it's
all part of the subconscious
pleasure we derive from
a day on the course.

Golf takes us to that universal yet irregular place where we all
experience its charms but no one can define them.

BILL COORE

Weather is just one of many things beyond a photographer's control. In pursuit of a pristine shot, first thing in the morning and last light in the evening are the best times to catch a golf course empty of players.

On this particular morning the sun had just tipped the horizon when a member of the ground staff arrived to mow the green. He wasn't there for long, but with all the elements in place it felt like an eternity. Eventually he moved off and I managed to capture the tremendous sense of spaciousness before conditions deteriorated.

It's not uncommon to see golfers in business suits, miles from the nearest course, making imaginary practice swings, and to hear them comment that golf is easier – and more enjoyable – without sticks and balls. Given the erratic nature of my own game this old throwaway line is very much a reality for me. But my lack of expertise with the sticks and balls is more than compensated for in the knowledge there can't be many pursuits to beat walking around an attractive landscape looking for potentially great greens and fairways – and then getting to build them.

BOB HARRISON

St Andrews Link's Scotland. Old Course, Hole 14, Par 5

At 5a.m. when the sky is leaden grey and you're driving to the golf course, it seems the whole world is sleeping – even the birds. You start to wonder why you didn't stay in bed as well. Then a sliver of clear sky appears on the horizon, a burst of morning sun bathes the fairway in brilliant light, and suddenly it's all worthwhile.

Pine Valley Golf Club,
USA. Hole 10, Par 3

Pine Valley is widely regarded
as the finest golf course in the
world – a golfing cathedral.
Reverence aside, the golfer is
reminded of its many
challenges by such earthy
place-names as the bunker at
the front of the 10th which
is fondly referred to as
'The Devil's Asshole.'

'The Zone'. . . I experienced it at Pine Valley this summer.
Got so caught up in the place that I got sunburn on my teeth. I remember
hitting great shots and some really bad ones, without a care for either.
I just couldn't stop smiling and laughing. That is 'The Zone' for me.
Falling in love with a golf course.

IAN ANDREW

Bandon Dunes Golf Resort,
USA. Pacific Dunes,
Hole 11, Par 3

Initially I was disappointed
with the hazy skyline. Then I
noticed how the diffused light,
softly melding sea and sky
together, created an ethereal
quality to what is usually a far
more dramatic scene. This way
the background complements
the golf hole rather than
distracting attention.

All architects design golf courses in the image of their own games, and Pacific Dunes is the perfect reflection of my own. Sometimes it's perfectly calm and sunny; other times the wind blows; and there are days when the fog rolls in and I can't see a thing. Even on those days, though, it's a great place to be.

TOM DOAK

I waited ages for this shot.
Then when the light was just
right and I was about to press
the shutter release a romantic
couple strolled into frame,
hand-in-hand – seemingly
oblivious to the large-format
camera, tripod, bags of
photographic equipment, and
me. They dallied for what
seemed like forever. Then just
as I was about to ask them to
move, they strolled off. Peace,
harmony, and healthy blood
pressure returned … phew!

I get upset over a bad shot just like anyone else.
But it's silly to let the game get to you. When I miss a shot I just
think what a beautiful day it is. And what pure fresh air I'm breathing.
Then I take a deep breath. I have to do that. That's what
gives me the strength to break the club.

BOB HOPE

Ballybunion Golf Club, Ireland. Hole 15, Par 3

It looks serene, but the clouds looming in the background promised bad weather on the way. My calm potterings turned to a mad rush and I grabbed this shot with only moments to spare before the sky broke.

Joondalup Resort, Australia. Quarry, Hole 3, Par 3

At the conclusion of the 2nd hole a cursory look at the card gives no hint of what's to come: a short par three. Only on arrival do you realise there's a great plunging quarry between the tee and the green – not so simple after all. The same goes for shooting it as I discovered when I tried to fill the frame with all those highly photogenic elements. To call it deceptive is an understatement.

Immaculate grooming subtly
illuminated by the final rays
of sunlight ... solitary scuff
marks in the bunker to indicate
the passage of a wayward
golfer ... a fitting epitaph
to a beautiful day.

Some days playing golf can be like sipping fine, aged,
red wine and other days it can be like crushing grapes.

IAN BAKER-FINCH

St Andrews Links,
Scotland. Old Course,
Hole 18, Par 4

Golf course and community
are intricately interwoven at
St Andrews. After all, this is
where the game began,
so the sense of history
envelopes you the instant
you enter the town. Every
serious golfer should
endeavour to make
the pilgrimage.

God has enabled me to understand that I'm at my personal best, my most coherent, when I'm on a golf course in the evening hours enjoying the game. Because there is no better time for me to understand just how special a gift life really is.

TOMMY NACCARATO

**Merion Golf Club,
USA. East Course,
Hole 9, Par 3**

I don't usually assign a
gender to a golf course,
but to me, Merion has an
unmistakable aura of
femininity. All subtle curves,
inimitable style, elegance
and grace. It's the Audrey
Hepburn of golf courses.
Beautiful to photograph
and beguiling to play.

Three things there are as unfathomable as they are fascinating to the
masculine mind: metaphysics, golf and the feminine heart.

ARNOLD HAULTAIN

Golf ... *it's a funny game*

We say we play it for pleasure and relaxation. But how can we explain the anger, the rage, the frustration, or the despair the game engenders?

'It's the challenge,' we chant.

But how often do we really meet that challenge? Occasionally we manage to smash the ball down the fairway. Clean as a whistle. Sweet as a breeze. Just like the Tiger. And occasionally it even lands pretty close to where we intended. Alas, more than occasionally we trudge, crestfallen, into that jungle called 'the rough' in a vain attempt to retrieve that *#@+*#@#* ball!

Then occasionally – and that's very, very, very occasionally – we stare in disbelief as a 50-foot putt drops into the hole. For some players this can be a cathartic moment. Their faith in a God of Golf is restored. Miracles still happen. And they cast their eyes towards the cosmos and give thanks.

But on far too many occasions we gaze in disbelief as that ineffable little ball – caringly and lovingly stroked along the gentlest twelve-inch journey of all time – glides past the hole, gathering speed as it goes. We've managed the impossible. We've missed the unmissable. Again!

That, as all golfers know, is the real cause of grey hair and baldness. Not advancing years or depleted hormones. Just bloody bad putting! It's as simple as that!

And then things go from bad to worse. Just to add 'interest' we make it even more difficult. 'What about a little wager? A round of drinks? A couple of bucks? Not a problem. Sure, I'll be in it!' Now, it's not just the ball that's lined up for a beating. It's the ego as well! And all aided and abetted by a twelve-inch, downhill, across-the-slope, into-a-force-10-gale putt. Is it any wonder we miss? Whose suggestion was it anyway?

But despite all these trials and tribulations we return to the battle again and again. Why? Because the next game will be the greatest we'll ever play. And sometimes it actually is! Sometimes the dream really does come true.

On the other hand it may be that golf is a kind of sporting meditation. A self-induced, trance-like state. Where all the hustle and bustle and day-to-day hassles are shut away in a little box at the back of the mind. Totally forgotten until we find ourselves back in our own driveway. Crash-landed back into reality by the sight of that great unkempt grassland we used to call 'the lawn.'

Or maybe it's something as simple as spending time with good friends. A few jokes. A few laughs. Indulging in the gentle art of gamesmanship. Or the genuine admiration of a shot well played. Followed, of course, by that all-important, expert, in-depth post-mortem at the 19th hole.

Or perhaps it's the salutary consolation that if all else fails ... there's always the view.

Golf ... it's a funny game.

FOLLOWING SPREAD The National Golf Club, Australia. Old Course, Hole 7, Par 3

Carne Golf Links,
Ireland. Hole 15, Par 4

An undiscovered gem and a
sheer delight to photograph.
The scenery is breathtaking and
the course itself is riddled with
challenges. With wild, wind-
swept dunes like this, it's
almost too easy finding a place
to set up my tripod.

Golf is a great sport for many reasons, not least of which is that it's the
only game where you call a penalty on yourself . . .

RICHIE BENAUD OBE

**Brora Golf Club,
Scotland. Hole 16, Par 4**

Brora is a links layout as
traditional as they come.
Sheep and cows roam the
fairways and rough, keeping
the grasses under control as
they have done for decades.
In the interest of smooth,
pristine greens, electric fences
surround the putting surface
to keep our pastoral friends at
bay. But generally, nature and
golf co-exist harmoniously
– apart from the occasional
bovine mini-stampede to
keep the players
on their toes.

Golf: A day spent in strenuous idleness.

WILLIAM WORDSWORTH

The Royal Melbourne Golf Club, Australia. West Course, Hole 6, Par 4

Seasonal changes can be crucial when you're dealing with the unique landscape of a golf course. It took a couple of months and several visits to get this shot, as towering trees on the right of the fairway cast deep shadows on the green, giving me no end of grief. As Summer turned to Autumn the sun began to shift further into the northern sky. Finally I had the conditions I'd been waiting for, and one morning this spectacular cloud formation appeared like a gift from God.

Most of the better spiritual moments for me on the course have come early in the morning when I've been alone. Something about being out there with nothing but your clubs, watching nature get ready for the day ahead, just makes you think profound thoughts.

DAN KING

Bandon Dunes Golf Resort, USA.
Bandon Dunes, Hole 16, Par 4

Words cannot express . . .

Royal Adelaide Golf Club
Australia. Hole 11, Par 4

It's not much fun taking
pictures in the heat. On
this occasion the serenity
of the image in no way
indicates the searing
temperature, nor the
frazzled, sweat-soaked
photographer toughing it
out behind the camera.

The magic of golf to me is the variety of moods it
can satisfy. The moments of reflection on a lonely course.
The test of skill and tingle of a pressure shot. The mateship and sidebets.
Tall stories and cool beers at the 19th hole. The variety of golf courses
with their different challenges and charms. The beautiful scenery
and connection with nature. This silly game called golf clears
my head, and urges on my soul.

GREG RAMSAY

Boat of Garten Golf Club,
Scotland. Hole 16, Par 4

On the evening I took this
photograph, a wind whipped up
so fierce it could have knocked
the spots off a Dalmatian. It was
all I could do to keep the tripod
steady. Aside from the wind,
let's not forget the other
quintessential Scottish
elements: tumbling banks of
heather and gorse, a haze of
silver birches, and the haunting
Cairngorm Mountains in
the background.

The least thing upset him on the links. He missed short putts because
of the uproar of butterflies in the adjoining meadows.

P. G. WODEHOUSE

**Kingston Heath Golf Club
Australia. Hole 15, Par 3**

Sitting around waiting for the
perfect light can be pretty
tedious. On this occasion the
sun was taking its time going
down, so when the course
superintendent came over for a
quick chat it was much
appreciated. A bit later he
returned to let me know the
automatic sprinkler system
would start at 7.30, which
turned out to be invaluable
advice. Not only would I have
been drenched and missed my
shot, but the potential damage
to my equipment could
have been disastrous.

If I were to interview for a job I would do everything in my
power not to disclose I golf or that it plays an important role in my life.
I think golfers are unproductive daydreamers who have a disdain for
overtime and working weekends.

JAKA B

Pelican Waters Golf Club, Australia. Hole 18, Par 4

It was the final morning of the Pelican Waters assignment and the pre-sunrise sky was overcast and threatening. Suddenly, a small chink opened up on the horizon. The 18th was the closest green I could get to so I frantically set up the camera and succeeded in getting a shot when the sun peeped through. Minutes later the heavens opened and a tropical downpour set in for the rest of the day.

Carne Golf Links, Ireland. Hole 11, Par 4

Carne is set among lofty sand dunes, with the back nine boasting the most impressive specimens. The tee shot on the 11th is truly awesome: curling around the base of a particularly massive dune. Here the picture possibilities are as sensational as the hole itself.

My timing was wayward and I had to sit around for quite some time waiting for the sun to set. Thoroughly rugged up with layers of warm clothes, I still couldn't stop shivering. Observing the locals in shorts and shirtsleeves I decided they must be completely impervious to cold ... or mad. Probably a little of both.

The Preserve Golf Club,
USA. Hole 7, Par 4

Perhaps the most aptly
named course in the world
with a journey of ten miles
from the security gate to
the actual golf course!

Charlie Brown isn't a golfer at all. He's a caddie. He caddies for Snoopy
because I think there's more money in it.

CHARLES M. SCHULZ

Merion Golf Club, USA. East Course, Hole 11, Par 4

Merion is a club with more than its fair share of golfing history. Ben Hogan hit his famous long iron shot to the 18th to join a play-off in the 1950 US Open. And during the 1930 US Open Bobby Jones clinched his golfing Grand Slam at the 11th. It's a privilege just to be there and an honour to photograph.

Golf is somewhere between a religion and a disease.

BILL 'REDANMAN' VOSTINAK

Bandon Dunes Golf Resort,
USA. Bandon Dunes,
Hole 15, Par 3

Relentless wind, cavernous
bunkers, rough spiteful
enough to swallow dinosaurs,
and scenery to distract the
most dedicated golfer. It's a
challenge for all players to
face the 15th at Bandon
Dunes and a pleasure for
any photographer.

As for golf . . . well, I am just in the 'lesson' phase. After two years
of working in this beautiful place, I decided to take the plunge and learn
the game. Right now, it's flashes of brilliance, followed by periods
of mediocrity. But I keep trying!

MARLA TAYLOR

Narooma Golf Club, Australia. Hole 3, Par 3

I'd long been fascinated from afar by the 3rd at Narooma. Images showed a spectacular hole with a terrifying tee shot that offered no chance whatsoever of retrieving a poor hit. The challenge seemed even more daunting the day I came to play it, with its green perched out on the point and gaping chasm before it, but luck was on my side. I parred the hole and took a photograph to be proud of.

Pebble Beach Golf Links, USA. Hole 8, Par 4

The 8th at Pebble Beach requires a knee-trembling second shot across the ocean to reach the green. Once you've navigated that obstacle, the heart rate slows down again, breathing becomes normal and you can take the time to appreciate the superb view.

I can tell right away if a guy is a winner or a loser just by the way he conducts himself on the course.

DONALD TRUMP

**The Heritage Golf and
Country Club, Australia.
St John Course, Hole 5, Par 4**

Seems my eyes are constantly
tuned to seek out the contrast
between a golf course and the
surrounding landscape. At the
Heritage the wide sweeping
fairways and rolling hills in the
background provide a
wonderfully divergent image
alive with colour. After a
number of attempts the
weather finally did what I was
hoping for and this vivid
palette emerged in all its glory.

To be out there in the middle of a game of golf is just the greatest.
You're inspired, you're eager, you're excited. Win or lose, I still feel
that way whenever I play the game.

JACK W. NICKLAUS

Ballybunion Golf Club,
Ireland. Hole 11, Par 4

There's more than one way to
play this hole. I started with an
horrendous hook from the tee
that I never expected to find
among the dunes. Then
somehow I managed to hit a
five iron on to the green and
take two putts for par, ending
up with a score that was little
short of a miracle. In hindsight
I can safely say it was an
undeserved outcome,
but oh-so very satisfying.

Golf drives us mad and keeps us sane. If its technical application
is our enemy, the courses are our refuge — great courses, scenic courses,
remote courses, challenging courses, tantalizing courses, widely
contrasting courses, courses that provide the great escape.
Without them, there would be no game.

DONALD STEEL

Acknowledgements

My sincere thanks goes to all who have contributed their thoughts about what makes golf special to them.

To Ian Baker-Finch, Richie Benaud, Bill Coore, Ben Crenshaw, Tom Doak, David Feherty, Bob Harrison, Greg Norman, Greg Ramsay, and Donald Steel who all took the time to think about their passion for the game and compose an original quote to appear in this book. I am forever grateful.

To the people who have given me permission to use their words taken from other sources. Muhammad Ali, Donald Trump, and the Estates of Bob Hope and Charles M. Schultz, I owe you all a debt of gratitude.

GolfClubAtlas.com led me to amusing and personal quotes from Ian Andrew, 'JakaB,' Dan King, Tommy Naccarato, and Bill 'redanman' Vostinak. My thanks to GolfClubAtlas.com for a forum that allowed me to find these words and a special thank you to the five gentlemen for kindly allowing me to reproduce their musings.

To Marla Taylor at Bandon Dunes Golf Resort for allowing me to use an excerpt from one of her emails to me.

To the Heritage Golf and Country Club for permission to use the excerpt of Jack Nicklaus.

To A.P Watt Ltd on behalf of the Trustees of the Wodehouse Estate. Wodehouse, P. G. *The Clicking of Cuthbert*. London; Herbert Jenkins Limited, 1922 and also from *The Clicking of Cuthbert* by P G Wodehouse, published by Hutchison. Reprinted by permission of The Random House Group Ltd.

To Gerard McCourt; where would I be without your word skills? Thank you Gerry for turning my ramblings to coherent text and for the ultimate polish given during the final editing.

To Jennifer Castles for the succinct caption writing.

To *Golfer Magazine* and editor Colin Sheehan.

To Nick Quin for the author's portrait. A great effort with such ordinary subject matter.

What would be the use of all the elements if they were not presented in an appropriate manner? My thanks to Andrew Cunningham of Studio Pazzo for once again dazzling me with his wonderful book designing skills.

And last, but certainly not least, to all the Golf Clubs depicted in this book. Without your cooperation and agreement this book would not have happened.

Every effort has been made to contact all copyright holders. Should there be any omissions we will be happy to rectify any mistakes in future editions.